UK Tax Questions and Answers

Global Guide 2016 – 2017

Dr Clifford J. Frank, LLM, PhD

Tax on Corporate Lending and Bond Issues

Dr Clifford J. Frank

UK Tax Questions and answers

Global Guide 2016 – 2017

Volume 2

Tax on Corporate Lending and Bond Issues in the UK

(England and Wales)

UK Tax Questions and Answers

Global Guide 2016 – 2017

Copyright © 2016 LEXeFISCAL LLP.

ISBN-13: 978-1533672605

ISBN-10: 1533672601

To my wife Marianna, who is always there for me.

Whilst the United Kingdom's highly competitive tax regime is one of the reasons why it is currently one of the best places in Europe and the world to do business it is, from a legal and regulatory perspective, a most challenging and bewildering jurisdiction for the uninitiated and for those seeking to either invest or do business in the UK or immigrate here.

The government is currently attempting formulate and implement a series of reforms aimed at tackling a wide variety of issues which impact upon business and the tax regime. These range from proposals to curb tax avoidance by removing a duty of care owed by employees to their employers if they choose to whistle-blow, to allowing HMRC to directly recover back taxes from the bank accounts of debtors and the much-publicised reforms on the non-dom. tax regime.

For those about to invest, immigrate or do business in the UK, this latest handbook from Dr Clifford J Frank provides a timely measure of support and essential guidance in these challenging and uncertain regulatory times.

Dr Frank is a highly experienced tax law practitioner, with more than 35 years' experience in International and UK Taxation, as well as the fields of arbitration, contract disputes and investment matters. I understand that he has worked in Europe for many years and is widely connected with associates working in the areas of international taxation and civil litigation. He has advised clients in a wide variety of complex civil and corporate litigations, including the merits of arbitrating before the ICSID and ICC, issues arising from the Insolvency Act 1986 and matters connected with capital raising, preparation of investment memorandum and pre-IPO. He has also recently acted as a tax attorney before the first tier tribunal in a complex MITIC case.

In this compact yet highly useful guide, Dr Frank deploys his considerable experience and expertise on the UK tax regime to provide a highly focused and user-friendly guide to lay clients and foreign practitioners alike. Written as a series of answers and expositions to frequently asked questions, the Global Guide 2016-2017 delivers a highly accessible overview to the UK tax regimes.

Lawrence Jones LL.B
Barrister at Law
Lincoln's Inn
May 2016

UK TAX QUESTIONS AND ANSWERS GLOBAL GUIDE 2016 – 2017

VOLUME 2

Tax on Corporate Lending and Bond Issues in the UK

Author: Dr Clifford J Frank, LLM, PhD

Created by: Marianna Penna

Contributor: Angelo Chirulli, ACA, CIPD

Design Contribution: Antonio Formisano

VOLUME 2

TAX ON CORPORATE LENDING AND BOND ISSUES IN THE UK (ENGLAND AND WALES)

Law at November 2015

Contributor: Angelo Chirulli, ACA, CIPD

OVERVIEW

A Q&A guide to tax on corporate lending and bond issues in the UK (England and Wales).

This Q&A provides a high level overview of finance tax in the UK and focuses on corporate lending and borrowing (including withholding tax requirements), bond issues, plant and machinery leasing, taxation of the borrower and lender when restructuring debt, securitisations, the Foreign Account Tax Compliance Act (FATCA) and bank levies.

To compare answers across multiple jurisdictions, visit the PLC Law Tax on Corporate Lending and Bond Issues: Country Q&A tool.

The Q&A is part of the global guide to tax on transactions. For a full list of jurisdictional Q&As visit www.practicallaw.com/taxontransactions-guide.

TAX AUTHORITIES

1. **What are the main authorities responsible for enforcing taxes on finance transactions in your jurisdiction?**

The main UK authority responsible for enforcing taxes on finance transactions is Her Majesty's Revenue & Customs (HMRC), a non-ministerial department of the UK Government responsible for the collection of UK taxes, the payment of some forms of state support, and the administration of other regulatory regimes (including the national minimum wage).

Pre-completion tax clearances

2. **Is it possible or necessary to apply for tax clearances from the tax authorities before completing a finance transaction?**

Circumstances for obtaining clearance

A taxpayer may wish to obtain confirmation from the tax authority as to the tax treatment of a particular transaction that is contemplated or has been carried out.

Taxpayers can apply for one of two types of clearances from HMRC:

- Statutory clearance, which concerns a specific point covered by tax law.
- Non-statutory clearance, which is where there is a material uncertainty as to how tax law applies to a particular transaction.

However, HMRC has always made it clear that no assurances concerning the tax treatment of a transaction will be given in any situation where, in HMRC's view, the arrangements constitute tax avoidance.

Mandatory or optional clearance?

Formal statutory clearance refers to certain statutory rulings and applications which HMRC must consider and respond to. They are available under specific statutory provisions and relate to particular types of arrangement. Usually, these are sought before a transaction is implemented. Formal statutory clearances are available under several statutory provisions, and are generally available to all taxpayers within the relevant charge to UK tax.

Where a formal statutory clearance is not available, HMRC may offer a non-statutory clearance (that is, a less formal ruling which is aimed at providing certainty in borderline tax cases). A non-statutory clearance is a written confirmation of HMRC's view of the application of tax law to a specific transaction or event that a taxpayer can rely on in most circumstances. This informal system is available to all "business customers".

Before using HMRC's clearance service, a taxpayer must first check that the transaction in question is not covered by a more appropriate clearance or approval route, and should check HMRC's guidance to see if the guidance provides an answer to the the relevant question.

A basic and important requirement, which applies to all clearance applications, is that the taxpayer must provide full and accurate disclosure of all relevant facts relating to the transaction. Any clearance given on the basis of incomplete or inaccurate disclosure will be void.

Procedure for obtaining clearance

Applications for both statutory and non-statutory clearances are submitted in letter form. Every applicant must ensure that all mandatory information required by the application is included.

Common clearance scenarios. Formal statutory clearance is requested mainly for qualifying life assurance policies, withholding tax (WHT) transactions in shares or debentures and transfer pricing (TP) issues. TP issues are specifically covered by advance pricing agreements. HMRC has run an advanced pricing agreements programme since 1999 to assist businesses in identifying solutions for complex TP issues.

The most common formal statutory clearances are those for:

- Share exchanges (*section 138, Taxation of Chargeable Gains Act 1992* (TCGA 1992)).
- Schemes of reconstruction (*sections 138 and 139(5), TCGA 1992*).

- Share buy-backs (*section 1045, Corporation Tax Act 2010 (CTA 2010)*).
- Demergers (*section 1091, CTA 2010*).
- Transactions in securities (*section 701, Income Tax Act 2007*).

Responses and reviews. HMRC must give a substantive response to clearance applications within 30 days of receipt.

Some of the clearance facilities, such as those for reorganisations and reconstructions and demergers (but not the transactions in securities rules), contain a right to request a review of the correspondence by the First-tier Tribunal (which should be done within 30 days of HMRC's decision). If the tribunal grants clearance, this is binding on HMRC.

Disclosure of finance transactions

3. Is it necessary to disclose the existence of any finance transactions to the tax authorities?

Circumstances where disclosure is required

If a taxpayer is involved in a tax avoidance scheme which has certain characteristics (called "hallmarks") which mean that the scheme must be disclosed under the disclosure rules, he must provide information about that scheme to HMRC.

This helps HMRC to:

+ Obtain early information about schemes and how they are claimed to work.
+ Find out quickly who has used a scheme.

If the taxpayer does not inform HMRC about a scheme that must be disclosed, he could be liable to a penalty. In addition, the promoter of a tax avoidance scheme relating to a finance transaction who does not disclose the scheme to HMRC under the Tax Avoidance Schemes (Information) Regulations 2004 will also be liable to a penalty.

Manner and timing of disclosure

There are two different disclosure regimes:

+ One for value added tax (VAT).
+ One for direct taxes and National Insurance contributions.

For VAT purposes, if a finance transaction creates a VAT advantage, the company must disclose this under the VAT (Disclosure of Avoidance Schemes) Regulations 2004.

Under the Disclosure of Tax Avoidance Schemes (DOTAS) regime, certain people must provide information to HMRC about tax avoidance schemes within five days of the schemes being made available or being implemented. Usually the person providing the information will be the promoter of the scheme (the person who designs or markets the scheme). He must make the disclosure within the five-day period.

The taxpayer is also obliged to disclose a tax avoidance scheme to HMRC within five business days (if there is an offshore tax avoidance scheme promoter) or 30 business days (if there is no scheme promoter) of entering into the first relevant transaction.

HMRC provides the promoter or the taxpayer with a unique reference number. The taxpayer must disclose this number on its tax return.

In particular cases, the UK National Crime Agency (NCA) must give consent for a financial transaction. On 9 September 2014, the National Crime Agency (NCA) updated a suspicious activity report (SAR) webpage on seeking consent for financial transactions under the Proceeds of Crime Act 2002 (POCA).

If there is a suspicion in relation to a transaction, the taxpayer is under a legal obligation to make the disclosure before the prohibited act takes place, and to obtain the appropriate consent from the NCA, to avoid liability in relation to the principal money laundering offences under POCA. Therefore, a new disclosure, which is different from the HMRC disclosure, will have to be submitted in these cases.

TAXES ON CORPORATE LENDING/BORROWING

Taxes potentially chargeable on amounts receivable

4. What are the main corporate taxes potentially chargeable on interest and other amounts receivable under a loan?

Corporation tax (loan relationship rules)

Key characteristics. Corporation tax is charged on interest and other amounts receivable under a loan. The amount of corporation tax that is charged is determined by the loan relationship rules.

For the purposes of the Corporation Tax Acts a company has a loan relationship if:

- The company stands in the position of a creditor or debtor as regards any money debt (whether by reference to a security or otherwise).
- The debt arises from a transaction for the lending of money.

Companies are generally taxable on the debits and credits that are recognised in their statutory accounts in respect of their loan relationships and related transactions. The legislation is specific about the debits and credits that are taxable, and the basis of the accounts that they are drawn from.

The term "loan relationship" also includes "relevant non-lending relationships" and certain other financing arrangements which are deemed to be loan relationships for tax purposes, but in these cases only certain debits and credits are within the scope to tax.

The term "related transaction" is defined in section 304 of the Corporation Tax Act 2009 (CTA 2009) as a disposal or acquisition (in whole or in part) of rights or liabilities under a loan relationship.

Triggering event. The loan relationship rules generally impose tax, and provide relief, in accordance with the accounting treatment of amounts arising in relation to loans, so it is accounting recognition that triggers tax or relief.

Calculation of tax. Profits arising from a company's loan relationships are taxed as income (*section 295, CTA 2009*), either as part of the company's trading profit or as non-trading income.

It is important to underline that the loan relationships regime generally takes precedence over other statutes unless there is an express provision to the contrary (*section 464, CTA 2009*). In addition to adjustments under the regime itself, the amounts charged to tax are subject to the transfer pricing, thin capitalisation and debt cap provisions. However, an amount which is denied relief under these rules is not generally deductible elsewhere.

The loan relationship rules operate by reference to amounts recognised by companies for accounting purposes. Those accounts must be prepared under generally recognised accounting practice (GAAP), including UK and International Accounting Standards (*section 1127, CTA 2010*).

Sections 307(3) and 307(4) of the CTA 2009 contain specific provisions concerning the nature of the debits and credits which a company must bring into account. They are the amounts that together fairly represent:

- All profits or losses from its loan relationships.
- Interest arising from its loan relationships.
- Expenses incurred by the company for the purpose of its loan relationships and related transactions, subject to certain restrictions as discussed in *Question 5*.

Section 308 of the CTA 2009 ensures that debits and credits are in charge to tax wherever they are booked, including in:

The profit and loss account, income statement or statement of comprehensive income.

The company's statement of recognised gains and losses, or statement of changes in equity.

Any other statement of items brought into account in calculating the company's profits and losses for the period.

As the loan relationship rules tax all profits and losses arising on a company's loan relationships, it is not usually necessary to determine whether a particular interest expense constitutes interest. However, some money debts will only be relevant non-lending relationships if they give rise to interest, and certain anti-avoidance measures (for example, governing late interest) only apply to interest. The Tax Acts do not contain a definition of interest and so the question of what constitutes interest relies on case law. HMRC guidance contains **a** useful discussion and highlights key principles from case law in HMRC's Corporate Finance Manual, at paragraph CFM33030. Several cases have highlighted the characteristic of interest as the compensation for the use of money over a period of time (*see Bennett v Ogston 15 T C 374; Wigmore v Thomas Summerson 9 T C 577; Willingale v International Commercial Bank 52 T C 242*). Certain amounts which are not interest are treated as such for the purpose of the loan relationship rules, including returns on repossessions and alternative finance arrangements.

Treatment of taxable amounts. Profits arising from a company's loan relationships are taxed as income rather than capital, and their classification as trading or non-trading is determined by how the funds are actually used.

Generally speaking, where a loan is used to generate income which is taxed as trading profits, it is a trading loan relationship under section 297 of the CTA 2009.

Debits and credits from non-trading loan relationships are pooled together, resulting in either a net credit or a net deficit. Where a company lends funds to an associate, it will generate non-trading loan relationship income unless lending is an integral part of its trade (*section 298,*

CTA 2009). This will only usually be the case for banks and financial institutions.

Connected party rules. The general rule in section 354 of the CTA 2009 is that no relief is available for a provision against, or a loss on writing off, a loan receivable from a connected party. Moreover, when parties cease to be connected, the lender may not claim relief for impairment losses booked in any subsequent period (*section 355, CTA 2009*). This is balanced by section 358 of the CTA 2009, which provides for a corresponding credit on the release of a connected party debt to be left out of a charge to tax.

"Connected" in this instance refers to the connection between the parties to a loan if they are both companies and the conditions of section 466 of the CTA 2009 are met. In particular, if the parties are connected at any time in an accounting period, they are held to be connected for the whole of that period. There is a connection if one party controls the other, or both fall under the common control of a third person. Control is defined in section 472 of the CTA 2009, and it is important to note that this definition requires the power of a person to secure that the affairs of a company are conducted in accordance with his wishes.

Anti-avoidance rules. The loan relationship regime contains a number of specific anti-avoidance measures concerned with deeming that loan relationships exist where funding transactions are structured in a way which would otherwise keep income out of the charge to tax, or tax it as capital (where it may be sheltered by capital losses). These rules are generally only come into play where deliberate structuring is being undertaken to mitigate tax, and they should be looked at closely in those circumstances.

Applicable rate(s). The corporation tax rate for company profits from 1 April 2015 is 20%.

Tax reliefs available for borrowing costs

5. **What corporate tax reliefs are available for borrowing costs (including interest and other amounts payable under a loan)?**

Corporation tax (loan relationship relief)

Key characteristics. Profits and losses arising from loan relationships, including from "related transactions" (including any loan relationship transfer, novation or assignment), are generally subject to UK corporation tax (or attract corporation tax relief) under the loan relationships legislation in Part 5 of CTA 2009 broadly in accordance with the accounting treatment show in the transferor's accounts.

Triggering event. The loan relationship rules generally impose tax, and provide relief, in accordance with the accounting treatment of amounts arising in relation to loans, so it is accounting recognition that triggers tax or relief.

Calculation of relief. Part 5 of the CTA 2009 sets out a list a list of borrowing costs that should be deductible for corporation tax purposes under the loan relationship rules, generally in accordance with their accounting treatment.

The debits and credits that are to be brought into account for the purposes of the loan relationships legislation are the debits and credits arising on each of a company's loan relationships for the accounting period. This includes the following:

- Profits and losses of the company which arise from the company's loan relationships and related transactions.
- Interest under the company's loan relationships.
- Expenses incurred by the company for the purpose of its loan relationships and related transactions, provided they are incurred directly in:
  - bringing any of its loan relationships into existence;
  - entering into or giving effect to any of its related transactions;
  - making a payment under any of its loan relationships or related transactions;
  - collecting amounts due under any of its loan relationships or a related transaction.

HMRC's Corporate Finance Manual, at paragraph CFM33060 includes a useful table of the type of expenses which HMRC considers allowable.

Under section 297(1) of Part 5 of the CTA 2009, in any accounting period that a company is a party to a loan relationship for the purposes of a trade it carries on, UK corporation tax deductions arising from its borrowing costs should be treated as an expense of that trade, and the debits in respect of the relationship for the period will be treated as expenses of the trade which are deductible in calculating those profits.

Where a loan relationship is entered into by a borrower otherwise than for the purposes of its trade, the difference in excess between the loan relationship debits and the loan relationship credits should give rise to a "non-trading deficit", which may be either:

- Set off against any profits in the relevant accounting period.
- Otherwise deducted in calculating the borrower's loss for the accounting period in question.

This loan relationship relief may be restricted if:

- The credits or debits relate to any amount falling, when paid, to be treated as a distribution.
- The loan relationship has an unallowable purpose.

If the interest is paid late, the relief can be deferred in some circumstances.

There are other provisions which may limit the tax relief that can be obtained for interest or other financial costs, including:

- Worldwide debt cap.

- Transfer pricing/thin capitalisation rules.
- Group mismatch rules.
- Arbitrage rules.

Applicable rate(s). The corporation tax rate from 1 April 2015 is 20%.

Worldwide debt cap

The worldwide debt cap rules provide an objective measure of the net financing expenses of the UK part of a group against the gross financing expenses of the worldwide group as a whole. The rules also contain a gateway test that compares the UK net debt of a group with the gross debt of the worldwide group. The general principle underpinning the worldwide debt cap is that UK corporation tax deductions for interest and other finance expenses (including the interest element in finance leases) claimed by members of a large group are restricted by reference to the group's consolidated external finance costs. It follows that identifying the entities that make up the worldwide group (being a group that is "large") and the UK part of that group is the key to the operation of the rules.

Transfer pricing/thin capitalisation rules

A company is said to be thinly capitalised when it has more debt than equity. Most thin capitalisation cases involve a company which has more debt than it could have borrowed on its own resources, because it is borrowing either from, or with the support of, connected persons.

These rules can apply to:

- Transactions between two companies under common control.
- Transactions between two company's management.
- In certain circumstances, where there is a 40% relationship between two companies.

These rules aim to prevent a parent company extracting profits from a subsidiary by financing the company with debt rather than equity. In the absence of these rules, a subsidiary could reduce or eliminate its taxable profits using the loan deduction.

Group mismatches

A "group mismatch scheme" arises where a group seeks to take advantage of differing accounting treatments for financial instruments and/or differing tax treatment of transactions as between companies in the same group. Broadly, such schemes involve a tax relief arising to one group company without a corresponding tax charge arising in another, meaning that the group incurs an overall tax loss without suffering an overall economic loss.

For the rules to apply, it is not necessary for there to be a tax advantage motive if a tax advantage is practically certain at the outset. Therefore, although a standard intra-group loan or derivative would be unlikely to fall within the rules, taxpayers (and advisers) must ensure that they give the rules due consideration in all intra-group cases. However, this will not be a problem in relation to genuine third party loans or derivatives, as these cannot cause asymmetry within a group.

Arbitrage rules

The arbitrage rules seek to address attempts to secure favourable tax treatment through the manipulation of varying tax rules in different countries. These rules are divided between:

- The deductions rules, which apply where a tax scheme increases a UK tax deduction for a hybrid entity (that is, an entity treated as tax transparent in one jurisdiction but opaque in another) to more than the entity would otherwise have been received in the absence of the scheme.
- The receipts rules, which address the relatively narrow circumstances where an amount that represents a contribution of capital is received by a UK resident company in a non-taxable form while creating a tax deduction in the paying company.

Tax payable on the transfer of debt

6. What corporate, transfer, stamp or other taxes are payable on the transfer of a debt under a loan?

Corporation tax

Key characteristics. See *Question 4, Corporation tax (loan relationship rule): Key characteristics.*

Calculation of tax. See *Question 4, Corporation tax (loan relationship rules): Calculation of tax.*

Triggering event. See *Question 4, Corporation tax (loan relationship rules): Triggering event.*

Applicable rate(s). See *Question 4, Corporation tax (loan relationship rules): Applicable rates.*

Stamp duty and stamp duty reserve tax

Key characteristics. A transfer of a debt is in principle liable to 0.5% stamp duty. An agreement to transfer a debt is in principle subject to SDRT in the same way as an agreement to transfer shares. However, provided the debt does not have certain offensive features, its transfer is exempt (this is known as the loan capital exemption). This exemption exists as of right, so the unstamped transfer can be sent direct to the registrar or company secretary (as appropriate).

The term "loan capital" is defined in section 78(7) of the Finance Act 1986 as meaning:

- Any debenture stock, corporation stock or funded debt, by whatever name known, issued by a body corporate or other body of persons (including a local authority), whether formed or established in the UK or elsewhere.
- Any capital raised by such a body, if the capital is borrowed or has the character of borrowed money, whether it is in the form of stock or otherwise.
- Stock or marketable securities issued by any non-UK government.
- Any capital raised under arrangements that fall within section 507 of the CTA 2009 (which replaced section 48A of the Finance Act 2005). These are "alternative" finance arrangements, commonly entered into as part of a sharia-compliant transaction.

Accordingly, most borrowings by companies constitute loan capital and the assignment by the lender is exempt from stamp duty and SDRT.

Calculation of tax. Stamp duty or SDRT will be charged on the amount of chargeable consideration paid. However, if the loan capital exemption applies, no stamp duty or SDRT will be payable.

If the loan capital carries a right of conversion into shares or other securities, or a right to the acquisition of other shares or securities at the time the transferring instrument is executed, the exemption does not apply. HMRC has confirmed that convertible loan capital is not outside the exemption where it is only convertible into other loan capital that does not carry offensive rights.

There are restrictions that prevent the loan capital exemption applying to quasi-equity:

- **Right to interest exceeding a reasonable commercial return.** The exemption does not apply to an instrument transferring loan capital if that loan capital carries, or has carried, at any time, whether previously or at the time of transfer, a right to interest that exceeds a reasonable commercial return.

- **Right to interest calculated by reference to business results.** The exemption does not apply if the loan capital carries, or has carried, at any time a right to interest that is calculated by reference to the results of a business or the value of property (for example, where interest rates are geared to the borrower's trading results, production achieved or the price of commodities). An exception is where the interest reduces when the results of the business improve or the value of any property increases (or vice versa), subject to the Finance Act 2008 provisions see below.

- **Right to repayment of an amount exceeding the nominal amount of capital.** The exemption does not apply if the loan capital carries, or has carried at any time, a right, on repayment, to an amount which exceeds the nominal amount of the capital, and is not reasonably comparable with what is generally repayable (in respect of a similar nominal amount of capital) under the terms of the issue of loan capital listed in the Official List.

The Finance Act 2008 provides that, in relation to documents executed on or after 22 July 2008, the loan capital exemption is not prevented from applying solely because a capital market investment is results-dependent, provided that the issuer is a debtor in a capital market arrangement and issuer of a capital market investment, and the interest is on limited recourse terms (*section 101, Finance Act 2008*).

In addition, section 154 of the Finance Act 2008 introduced provisions to apply the loan exemption from stamp duty to transfers of certain types of loan capital raised under alternative finance arrangements falling within section 48A of the Finance Act 2005 (now rewritten into section 507 of the CTA 2009, commonly entered into as part of a sharia-compliant transaction).

Triggering event. Transfers of stock and marketable securities between companies in the same group potentially give rise to stamp duty in the same way as sales between unconnected parties. A person will pay SDRT on paperless transactions when they buy:

- Shares in a UK company.
- Shares in a foreign company with a share register in the UK.
- An option to buy shares.
- Rights arising from shares already owned.
- An interest in shares, such as an interest in the money made from selling them.

Liable party/parties. The SDRT legislation principally makes the buyer liable to pay.

Applicable rate(s). Stamp duty and SDRT are charged at 0.5% of the chargeable consideration paid.

Withholding tax

7. Is there withholding tax on interest or any other payments under a loan?

When withholding tax applies

Unless an exemption applies, where a payment of yearly interest has a UK source, an amount equal to the basic rate (currently 20%) of the payment must be withheld and, subject to set off, paid to HMRC.

Broadly, yearly interest is any interest on a loan or debt obligation that has a term of, or is intended to last for, at least a year (this includes any loan the duration of which is shorter than a year, but which is capable of being rolled over into one or more successive loans which, together, could exceed a year). The intention of the parties to a loan or debt obligation is key to determining whether or not interest is yearly interest, and therefore whether or not UK tax must be deducted from the payment.

If the interest does not have a UK source, there is no withholding requirement.

Applicable rate(s) of withholding tax

The current rate of withholding is 20% (not including any reduction or elimination of withholding tax by double tax treaties).

Exemptions from withholding tax

The exemptions commonly relied on to ensure that UK source payments made by companies can be made free from withholding tax include:

- Ensuring that the interest is short interest (that it, it is not yearly interest).

- The Eurobond exemption (a Eurobond is a security, issued by a company, which carries interest and is listed on a recognised stock exchange), which enables interest to be paid without the deduction of UK tax in respect of bonds listed on a recognised stock exchange.

- The UK to UK exemption, where at the time of making the payment, the payer reasonably believes that the recipient beneficially entitled to the payment is either:
    - a UK tax resident company;
    - a non-UK tax resident company for which the interest is within the charge to UK corporation tax in respect of its UK permanent establishment; or
    - a partnership, each member of which is either a UK tax resident company or a UK permanent establishment of a non-UK tax resident company.

- The exemption for interest paid by banks in the ordinary course of their business (which does not include interest on borrowings which relate to a bank's capital structure or are primarily attributable to an intention to avoid tax).

- Relying on a relevant double tax treaty to provide that interest can be paid gross to the relevant recipient.
- The lender is a 25% associate of the borrower and is liable to tax in another EU member state on the interest and HMRC has previously issued an exemption notice.

Guarantees

8. Do any particular tax issues arise on the provision of a guarantee?

If the guarantor made a payment under a loan guarantee, it is deductible only if both:

- The guarantee, when it was made, was wholly and exclusively for the purposes of the trade.
- A capital advantage is not secured by it.

A guarantee payment is likely to fail the wholly and exclusively test where either:

- There is no trading relationship between the guarantor and the person covered by the guarantee.
- The guarantee was given for the purpose of a non-trading relationship, such as that of associate of, or investor in, the guaranteed person.

If the guarantee is not given during the course of a trade, the position on whether or not the deduction can apply is much less clear. Under the "non-lending relationship" rules (part of the loan relationship rules), it may be possible to claim a deduction depending on the facts in each case.

Under the UK's thin capitalisation rules (part of the transfer pricing rules), a loan or credit guarantee is an agreement by the parent company (the guarantor) to pay any missing payments to an unrelated third party lending in the event its subsidiary (the borrower) defaults on its loan obligation. The key transfer pricing issue is whether the subsidiary (the borrower) should pay a guarantee fee (or other compensation) to its parent company, since the guarantee helped it obtain the third-party loan on favourable terms.

Under the thin capitalisation rules, the existence of the guarantee by an entity associated with the borrower may lead to tax denial of deductions for interest payments by the borrower to the extent that the borrowing is deemed to exceed the amount that could have been borrowed by the borrower on a stand-alone basis: A claim under section 192 of the Taxation (International and Other Provisions) Act 2010 may provide corporation tax deductions for UK guarantors in relation to amounts for which the borrower has had deductions disallowed.

Finally, depending on the terms of the loan agreement and guarantee, and any applicable double tax treaty, the amount of any guarantee fee paid by or to a non-resident may be subject to a special type of withholding tax. If interest payments are subject to interest withholding tax, then a payment by the guarantor in relation to defaulted interest may also be subject to withholding tax.

BOND ISSUES

9. For corporate taxation purposes, are bonds treated any differently from standard corporate loans?

In the UK investment bond gains are subject to income tax for individuals, personal representatives and trustees (*Chapter 9, Income Tax (Trading and Other Income) Act 2005* (ITTOIA 2005)). Where the policyholder is a company, then the loan relationship rules apply instead and they are not treated differently from standard corporate loans, and the same rules regarding UK corporation tax apply.

Taxes payable on the issue and/or transfer of a bond

10. What stamp, transfer or similar taxes are payable on the issue and/or transfer of a bond?

Bearer instrument duty (BID), stamp duty and SDRT

Issue of bearer bonds. BID is a duty that is charged on an *ad valorem* basis on:

* The issue in the UK of a bearer bond.
* The issue outside the UK of a bearer bond by or on behalf of a UK company.

- The first transfer in the UK of any other bearer bond (if stamp duty would be chargeable on an instrument effecting that transfer).

BID is charged at a rate of 1.5% of the issue price.

BID can be avoided on the issue of bearer bonds if a bearer bond is (*schedule 15, Finance Act 1999*):

- Not issued in the UK.
- Not issued by or on behalf of a UK company.
- Not subsequently transferred in the UK.

Transfer of bearer bonds. On the first transfer in the UK of the bearer bond, BID is payable at 1.5% of the transfer consideration only if:

- No BID was payable (or paid) on issue.
- Stamp duty (under paragraph 4, schedule 15 of the Finance Act 1999) would have been payable on the transfer if the bond had been in registered form.

Stamp duty is charged at a rate of 0.5% of the consideration for transfers of a bond if the bond was exempt from BID on issue (*paragraph 3, schedule 13, Finance Act 1994 and section 87, Finance Act 1986*).

Issue of registered bonds. Registered bonds are potentially subject only to stamp duty and SDRT, not BID. Subject to the special regime for issues into a depository or clearing system (see below), there is generally, no charge to stamp duty or SDRT on the issue of a registered bond.

Transfer of registered bonds. The transfer of a registered bond potentially gives rise to a stamp duty charge (at a rate of 0.5%) if the transfer is executed in the UK, or relates to UK stock or marketable securities or to something done, or to be done, in the UK. Any agreement to transfer a registered bond issued by a UK issuer or registered in a UK register will give rise to SDRT.

However, there will be no stamp duty or SDRT charge if the bonds constitute exempt loan capital (*see Question 11*) (if a bond constitutes exempt loan capital, it is not subject to any stamp duty, BID or SDRT on issue or transfer under section 79 of the Finance Act 1986). There will also be no SDRT charge if the bonds are issued by a non-UK incorporated company and registered in a register outside the UK. There should, therefore, be no stamp duty or SDRT if the transfer is executed outside the UK and has no UK nexus.

In addition, if a liability to stamp duty has in fact been triggered, it may, in practice, be unnecessary to pay the stamp duty unless the transfer is required to be adduced in evidence in legal proceedings, or the company registrar will not acknowledge the change in ownership affected by that transfer if the stamp duty is not paid.

Transfer of bonds into clearance services or depositary receipt arrangements. A stamp duty or SDRT charge of 1.5% arises on any transfer of bonds to a person (or the agent or nominee of such a person) whose business is, or includes, issuing depositary receipts or providing clearance services for chargeable securities (*sections 67 and 70, Finance Act 1986*).

The charge is based on:

* The issue price, in the case of an issue.
* The consideration, in the case of a transfer for consideration. If there is no consideration, the charge is based on the market value of the bonds.

Subsequent transfers of bonds within clearance services and dealings in depositary receipts are, generally, exempt from stamp duty and SDRT.

Exemptions

11. Are any exemptions available?

If a bond constitutes exempt loan capital, it is not subject to any stamp duty, BID or SDRT on issue or transfer (*section 79, Finance Act 1986*).

For the definition of "loan capital", see *Question 6*.

Bonds only need to be loan capital to be exempt from BID, but need to be "exempt" loan capital to be exempt from stamp duty and SDRT.

To be "exempt" loan capital, the bonds must not:

- Be convertible into, or carry a right to the acquisition of, shares or other securities. (Note, however, that loan capital is still exempt loan capital if it carries a right of conversion into, or the acquisition of, loan capital that itself falls within the exemption, as confirmed by HMRC in its Statement of Practice 3/84.)
- Carry a right to interest the amount of which exceeds a reasonable commercial return on the nominal amount of the capital.
- Carry (or have carried) a right to interest, the amount of which falls to be determined, to any extent, by reference to the results of a business, or any part of a business, or to the value of any property.

However, this does not prevent loan capital from being exempt if either:

- The interest is determined by reference to a UK domestic general prices index, such as the retail prices index (RPI) (but not if the returns are linked to FTSE or other equity indices).
- The rate of interest decreases in the event of the results of the business improving or the value of the property increasing, or increases in the event of the results of the business deteriorating or the value of the property decreasing.

BID is also not payable on the issue or transfer of a bearer bond outside the UK which is in the form of a foreign currency and not offered for transfer or subscription in the UK.

If a transfer is executed outside the UK with no UK connection, no stamp duty applies. There is no SDRT charge if the bonds are bearer bonds that are denominated in sterling or that are denominated in a foreign currency (raising new capital). The current position is that HMRC will not collect SDRT on the issue, or (where integral to the raising of capital) the transfer, of bonds into a clearing system or depositary receipt system, provided that the bonds comprise loans raised by the issue of debentures or other negotiable securities for the purposes of Article 5(2)(b) of the Capital Duty Directive (2008/7/EC).

PLANT AND MACHINERY LEASING

Claiming capital allowances/tax depreciation

12. What are the basic rules for enabling the lessor or lessee of plant and machinery to claim capital allowances/tax depreciation?

In very general terms, a lease that is accounted for as a finance lease and has a term of at least five years will be categorised as a "long funding lease", with other leases categorised as non-long funding leases.

The basic requirements to support a lessor's claim to capital allowances under a non-long funding lease of plant and machinery are that:

- The lessor must incur capital expenditure, that is, expenditure on an asset intended for long-term use in the lessor's business (as opposed to revenue expenditure on assets intended for resale).
- The asset must be plant and machinery.
- The lessor must incur the expenditure. At its simplest, this means that the lessor must lay out (or be obliged to lay out) money on the provision of the equipment.
- The lessor must incur the expenditure wholly and exclusively for the purposes of a trade (or other type of business activity specified in section 15 of the Capital Allowances Act 2001 (CAA 2001)). For the majority of established lessors, this is not likely to give rise to any issue.

• As a result of incurring expenditure, the asset must belong to the lessor. The lessor must be the beneficial owner of the equipment as a result of incurring the expenditure. However, where the expenditure is incurred under a deferred purchase arrangement, such as a hire-purchase or conditional sale agreement, special rules deem the asset to belong to the person having the benefit of that contract and the right to call for title (*section 67, CAA 2001*). Mere legal ownership (such as the holding of title by way of security) is not sufficient for capital allowance purposes.

Leases that are hire-purchase transactions, and leases of plant and machinery that is fixed or installed on to land where the plant and machinery is of a kind that would ordinarily be installed, and the sole or main purpose of which is to contribute to the functionality of a building or its site (known as "background plant and machinery"), are examples of leases which will be treated as non-long funding leases of plant and machinery. Most leases of ships to companies within the UK's tonnage tax regime and leases of a term of not more than five years are also considered to be non-long funding leases.

Capital allowances can be claimed by a lessee under a long funding lease of plant and machinery.

Rate of capital allowances /tax depreciation

13. What is the rate of capital allowances/tax depreciation; does it depend on the type of assets?

A taxpayer can claim capital allowances when he buys assets that he keeps to use in his business, for example:

+ Equipment.
+ Machinery.
+ Business vehicles (for example, cars, vans or lorries).

These are known as "plant and machinery".

A taxpayer can deduct some or all of the value of the item from his profits before he pays tax. In most cases he can deduct the full cost of these items from his profits before tax using the annual investment allowance (AIA).

A taxpayer can claim AIA up to a total of GB£500,000 on plant and machinery. If a taxpayer spends more than GB£500,000 he can claim writing down allowances on any amount above GB£500,000. If a single item takes a taxpayer above GB£500,000, he can split the value between the types of allowance.

A taxpayer cannot claim AIA on:

+ Cars.
+ Items owned for another reason before the taxpayer started using them in his business.
+ Items given to the taxpayer or his business.

A taxpayer can claim "writing down allowances" instead of AIA.

The rate of the writing down allowance for plant and machinery in the general pool is 18% from 1 April 2012.

A special rate pool exists for:

Thermal insulation added to an existing non-residential building.

"Long life assets" (broadly, plant and machinery with an expected useful economic life, when new, of 25 years or more).

Plant and machinery which qualifies as an "integral feature" (set out in section 33A of the CAA 2001).

The rate of writing down allowance for plant and machinery in the special rate pool is 8% from 1 April 2012.

There are 100% first-year "enhanced capital allowances" for qualifying expenditure incurred on energy saving and environmentally beneficial plant and machinery.

If a taxpayer buys an asset that qualifies for enhanced allowances he can deduct the full cost from his profits before tax. A taxpayer can claim enhanced allowances in addition to annual investment allowance, as they do not count towards the AIA limit.

Lessees not carrying on business in the jurisdiction

14. Are there special rules for leasing to lessees that do not carry on business in your jurisdiction?

For leases entered into on or after 1 April 2006, where plant and machinery is leased to a lessee who is not a UK resident for tax purposes who does not use the equipment solely for the purposes of its UK trade, capital allowances will be available to the lessee provided that both (*section 110, CAA 2001*):

- The equipment is leased to a lessee resident in the European Economic Area (EEA).
- The state where the lessee is resident in the EEA gives the lessee a relief that is broadly equivalent to capital allowances.

Under section 109 of the CAA 2001, the rate of available capital allowances is restricted to 10%.

If the state where the lessee is resident does not give the lessee a relief that is broadly equivalent to capital allowances, the lessor can claim capital allowances at the normal rate.

Taxation of rentals

15. How are rentals taxed?

If the lease is a long funding lease, the taxation of the lessor will depend on whether the lease is a finance lease or an operating lease, following the effect of the long funding lease regime introduced by the Finance Act 2006 (FA 2006).

Long funding leases to which the new rules apply are leases with a term of more than five years, or in some cases more than seven years.

Where the finance lease is a long funding lease the tax treatment follows the substance, and so the accounting treatment, of the transaction. If the lease is a finance lease, under section 360 of the CTA 2010 the lessor will normally be taxed on the total amount of rental earnings in respect of the lease for the relevant accounting period.

The rental earnings amount is the gross return on investment recognised in an accounting period in respect of the lease in accordance with GAAP. If the lease is considered as a loan by the lessor, any rentals which are deemed from an accountancy point of view as interest in an accounting period are still taxed as rental earnings.

An operating lease is a lease whose term is short compared to the useful life of the asset or piece of equipment being leased (for example, an airliner, a ship, and so on). If the lease is an operating lease, the lessor will be taxed on its rental income less a deduction equal to the expected gross reduction in value of the asset over the term of the lease which is attributable to the relevant accounting period.

Under sections 363 to 365 of the CTA 2010, the deduction represents a straight-line depreciation from the cost of the plant and machinery to its residual value over the term of the lease, allocated to each accounting period during the term of the lease.

Where the lease is not a long funding lease, for tax purposes the finance lessor has leased the asset to the lessee for a revenue hire charge. As a result, the gross rentals due under a finance lease ("interest" plus "capital" repayments) are all on revenue account. The gross rentals are:

- All taxable as income in the hands of the finance lessor (the capital cost of the leased asset may qualify for capital allowances, and in a plant or machinery case the cost of the asset should normally equal the capital element in the rentals).
- Deductible as revenue expenses in the hands of the finance lessee to the extent that the leased asset is used for the lessee's trade.

Rulings and clearances

16. Is a ruling or clearance necessary or common?

It is not mandatory to obtain any ruling or clearance from HMRC in relation to plant and machinery leasing.

RESTRUCTURING DEBT

Unpaid or deferred interest or capital

17. What is the tax treatment of the borrower and the lender if interest or capital is unpaid or deferred?

In general, if interest or capital are unpaid or deferred, for borrower will be entitled to a tax deduction (loan relationship debit), and creditors will recognise a taxable receipt (loan relationship credit), for amounts accruing in their accounts. The general approach of the loan relationship rules (governing the corporation tax treatment of loans) is to look to the parties' accounts rather than to actual payment.

Pursuant to sections 372 and 373, CTA 2009, the borrower will not obtain a loan relationship debit for interest until it is actually paid by him if both:

+ The debt is between "connected" parties but the interest is not paid within 12 months of the end of the accounting period in which it arises in the borrower's accounts.

- The full amount of the interest is not brought into account for corporation tax purposes by the lender.

As a result of amendments made by the Finance Act 2009, this deferral of relief for late paid interest until the time of payment applies only if either:

- The debtor controls the creditor, or vice versa, or both are under the control of a third person.
- The borrower has a major interest in the lender, or vice versa.
- The borrower is a "close company" and the creditor is a participator (or an associate of a participator).

In all of these cases, the lender must be either resident in a "non-qualifying territory" or effectively managed by its board in a "non-taxing non-qualifying territory" (that is, a territory with which the UK does not have a double tax treaty containing a non-discrimination article).

If a debt security is issued at a discount, rather than being interest bearing, pursuant to sections 406 to 412 of the CTA 2009, the debtor's loan relationship debits in respect of the discount may be deferred until the accounting period in which the discounted security is redeemed.

For lenders accounting for a loan on an amortised cost basis as opposed to a fair value basis, a loan relationship debit should be permitted for recognised accounting impairment losses (such as losses arising on a write-off or waiver of the debt, or if the debt is otherwise recognised in the lender's accounts as being a bad debt).

A lender, as a general rule exception, may not bring into account a loan relationship debit in respect of an impairment loss where at any time in the accounting period of the release the parties are connected; see *Question 18* in relation to debt for equity swaps and further details of releases or write-offs of debts.

Debt write-off/release and debt for equity swap

18. What is the tax treatment of the borrower and lender if a loan is: Written off or released (wholly or partly)? Replaced by shares in the borrower (debt for equity swap)?

Writing off or release

The effects of the writing off or release of a loan (in whole or in part) are:

- A taxable receipt (loan relationship credit) for the borrower.
- A corresponding tax deduction (loan relationship debit) for the lender.

The amounts released or written off will be considered in the accounts of the borrower as a profit and in those of the lender as a loss.

This general rule does not apply where an amortised cost basis of accounting as opposed to a fair value basis is applied to a loan in the relevant accounting period if one of the following conditions applies:

- There is a connection between the borrower and the lender in the relevant accounting period.
- The release is part of a "statutory insolvency arrangement" *(section 1319 of the CTA 2009)*.
- The lender:
    - is the subject of insolvent administration, insolvent liquidation or other insolvency procedures *(section 357, CTA 2009)*; and
    - was, immediately before the insolvency procedure, connected with the borrower, but immediately after the insolvency was not connected with the borrower *(section 359, CTA 2009)*.
- The borrower is the subject of an insolvency procedure *(section 322(6), CTA 2009)* and the parties are not connected *(section 322(5), CTA 2009)*.
- Pursuant to section 322(4), CTA 2009 The release is in consideration of an issue of ordinary share capital by the borrower *(section 322(4), CTA)*.

In these cases, a borrower should not recognise a loan relationship credit in respect of the release (although the lender should not benefit from a loan relationship debit in respect of the release).

Debt for equity swap

A borrower will not be required to bring into account a loan relationship credit where it is released from its obligations under a loan if both of the following conditions are met:

- The release is in an accounting period for which an amortised cost basis of accounting is used.
- Under section 322(4) of the CTA 2009, the debt is released "in consideration of" the issue of ordinary shares (and does not amount to a mere release of a debt).

The lender should be able to obtain a loan relationship debit equal to the amount by which the carrying value of the loan exceeds the market value of the loan on the date of the debt for equity swap if the swap is on the basis of that market value, as this is the loss that the lender will recognise in its accounts beyond the amount for which it has received shares from the borrower.

However, no loan relationship debit can be brought into account if the borrower and lender are connected before the debt for equity swap.

SECURITISATION

19. **Briefly explain the key features of the tax regime applicable to securitisations, including details of any specific tax rules that apply or issues that arise in relation to securitisations.**

A true sale securitisation (by virtue of its nature) necessarily entails a sale of assets by the originator group to the special purpose vehicle (SPV) issuer. These assets generally fall within one of three categories:

+ **Real estate.** There is likely to be a disposal of a capital asset for chargeable gains purposes (for example, the disposal of a freehold interest in a property subject to a lease). This can give rise to tax on a chargeable gain for the originator. There may also be a charge to stamp duty land tax. If the originator and the SPV issuer form part of the same group, it is possible that these charges may be relieved under the chargeable gains grouping and stamp duty land tax group relief provisions, respectively.

+ **Loan relationship assets.** These types of assets include:
    - mortgage loans;
    - bank loans to companies;
    - credit card receivables; and
    - other commercial loans.

The proceeds of the sale are assessed to tax in the originator group broadly in accordance with their recognition for accounting purposes (assuming that they accord with GAAP). For example, if the loans were sold at par together with deferred consideration, the timing of recognition of the profit element (that is, the deferred consideration) would depend on how that deferred consideration was recognised for accounting purposes.

- **Other receivables.** These are typically ordinary trade receivables (for example, the receivables of a utility company or a mobile telephone operator). Accordingly, the consideration for a sale is normally subject to tax for the originator as part of its ordinary trading profits.

However, it is possible that HMRC may argue that, for UK tax purposes, the originator should be deemed to have received market value for the receivables (if this is greater than the actual consideration) on the basis that the transfer is not in the ordinary course of the originator's trade and, therefore, falls within Chapter 10 of Part 3 of the CTA 2009.

Section 30 of the Finance Act 2014 (which inserts section 1035A into the CTA 2009) provides that if the profits of a group company are, in substance, transferred to a different group company, and a main purpose of that is to secure a tax advantage, the transfer is ignored for the purposes of calculating the transferor company's (but not the transferee's) corporation tax. This measure applies to payments made on or after 19 March 2014.

Depending on the nature of the asset transferred, the originator may be liable for VAT or stamp duties in respect of the sale.

The tax treatment of the SPV issuer will depend on whether it is taxed under the Taxation of Securitisation Companies Regulations 2006 (*SI 2006/3296*) (Securitisation Regulations 2006) or under general UK corporation tax principles.

As a result of the benefits of being taxed under the Securitisation Regulations 2006, most true sale securitisations will be structured in order to fall within these regulations where this is possible. The Securitisation Regulations 2006 provide (subject to certain conditions) a distinct tax regime with specific rules for securitisation companies. The regulations have effect for periods of account beginning on or after 1 January 2007 (subject to making an election in the case of certain companies existing at 31 December 2006).

Broadly, in order to fall within this tax regime, the SPV issuer must:

+ Qualify as a "securitisation company".
+ Satisfy the "payments condition" at all times (requiring the SPV issuer to pay out all of its income within a specified period other than profits and other amounts that it is required to obtain).
+ Not have an "unallowable purpose" at any time.

If a securitisation company satisfies the above mentioned conditions, it is subject to tax on its retained profit:

- Less any distributions received from other securitisation companies that are part of the same capital market arrangement (if paid out of that company's retained profit).
- Plus (if positive) the amount of any dividends paid by the company representing amounts not already taken into account (whether as dividends received, retained profit or otherwise) under the Securitisation Regulations 2006 in any accounting period.

This is subject to a minimum of zero. If a company does not have enough funds to retain as much profit as it intended under the securitisation structure, the company is taxed only by reference to the actual retained profit and the shortfall can be made good by being added to a later period's retained profit and taxed accordingly (*regulation 10, Securitisation Regulations 2006*).

It should be noted that if a securitisation company satisfies the conditions, it will automatically be subject to the tax treatment described above, as no election into the regime is required by the securitisation company (other than in the case of securitisation companies existing on 1 January 2007).

There is no opportunity for securitisation SPVs to test the scope of the payments condition and the unallowable purpose rule. This means that securitisation companies must be absolutely certain that they fall within the regime from its inception.

Under the Securitisation Regulations 2006, interest paid by a securitisation company is not treated as a distribution for UK tax purposes if it otherwise would be.

This exclusion from distribution treatment should not affect securitisation companies, as they are taxed only on their retained profit and so do not need any tax deductions. The real effect of the provision is on the position of the recipient.

For the purposes of Part 5 of the CTA 2010, a securitisation company cannot be treated as a member of any group or consortium (*regulation 17, Securitisation Regulations 2006*), and is therefore unable to make a claim for group relief or consortium relief. Conversely, certain provisions imposing secondary tax liablities may still apply to it. Additionally, even though limited recourse interest payable by an SPV issuer might not have adverse direct tax consequences for that SPV issuer, the stamp duty and SDRT position on a transfer of the debt must still be considered.

Where a securitisation company falls outside of the scope of the Securitisation Regulations 2006, it will be taxed in accordance with its accounts, which can give rise to uncertainty and potential increased tax costs that can, in turn, negatively affect anticipated cashflows.

FOREIGN ACCOUNT TAX COMPLIANCE ACT (FATCA)

20. Has your jurisdiction entered into an intergovernmental agreement (IGA) to implement FATCA, or do you intend to enter into an IGA to implement FATCA?

A model IGA was developed and published in July 2012. The UK and the US signed an IGA (the "UK-US Agreement to Improve International Tax Compliance and to Implement FATCA" (FATCA IGA)) in September 2012.

Annex II of the FATCA IGA was amended by an exchange of notes between the two governments (dated 3 June 2013 and 7 June 2013).

The FATCA IGA reduces some of the administrative burden of complying with the US regulations, and provides a mechanism for UK financial institutions to comply with their obligations without breaching UK data protection laws.

21. Have there been any particular difficulties in light of your jurisdiction's domestic legislation with implementing the FATCA requirements?

No particular difficulties have been encountered, although delays have occurred. On 12 July 2013 the US announced a delay of six months before the commencement of FATCA. The effect of this delay is that there has been no reporting with regard to 2013.

On 6 May 2014 the US announced amendments to the processes for new entity accounts opened between 1 July 2014 and 31 December 2014. The UK did not adopt these amendments. Therefore, where UK financial institutions are required to obtain self-certification for a new customer, the current processes have applied from 1 July 2014. This maintains consistency between the due diligence requirements imposed on UK entities for US and Crown Dependency/Gibraltar reporting purposes.

22. Are there any provisions of your jurisdiction's IGA and/or domestic implementing legislation, if any, that are more onerous than the US FATCA requirements?

The provisions of the UK's FATCA IGA are becoming more onerous. On 24 March 2015, the International Tax Compliance Regulations 2015 (*SI 2015/878*) (Compliance Regulations) were made, implementing the UK's agreements and arrangements on the exchange of tax information.

The Compliance Regulations require UK financial institutions to:

* Perform the due diligence obligations set out in the FATCA IGA, the Directive on Administrative Co-operation (DAC) and the Common Reporting Standard (CRS) (each a relevant agreement) to identify account holders that are resident overseas.
* Maintain a record of the due diligence.
* Report to HMRC those accounts identified as reportable to a jurisdiction where an exchange requirement exists. Schedule 1 to the Compliance Regulations lists the CRS participating jurisdictions.

The Compliance Regulations effectively unify, as far as possible, the due diligence and reporting requirements and penalties in relation to each relevant agreement. They have effect:

* For FATCA purposes, from 15 April 2015.
* For the DAC and the CRS, from 1 January 2016.

BANK LEVIES

23. Are there any bank levies or similar taxes imposed specifically on financial institutions?

In the June 2010 Budget, the UK government announced the introduction of a bank levy from 1 January 2011. The purpose of the levy is to make UK-based banks contribute at a level that reflects the risk that bank failure poses to the UK financial system and to the wider economy. It is intended to encourage banks to move away from riskier funding and is expected to raise about GB£2.5 billion per year from 2012. The government does not intend to use the revenue generated to set up a bail-out fund for the banking sector.

24. On what are any such levies or taxes charged?

The levy applies from 1 January 2011 and it is chargeable on:

- The global consolidated balance sheets of UK banking and building society groups.
- In relation to foreign banking groups, the aggregated balance sheets of UK sub-groups and UK subsidiaries, together with a proportion of the balance sheets of foreign banks with a UK permanent establishment.

- In relation to non-banking groups, the balance sheets of UK banks and banking sub-groups.
- The balance sheets of UK banks and building societies that are not members of groups.
- In relation to a foreign bank that is not a member of a group and has a UK permanent establishment, a proportion of its balance sheet.

However, from 1 January 2021, the levy is to be restricted to UK balance sheets of UK headquartered banks.

The bank levy is based on the chargeable equity and liabilities of the group or entity at the end of the chargeable period. The levy is charged on chargeable equity and liabilities to the extent that these exceed GB£20 billion.

25. At what rate(s) are the levies or taxes charged?

Different rates apply to:

- Short-term liabilities.
- Long-term equity and liabilities.

The rates are 0.21% (short-term liabilities) and 0.105% (long-term equity and liabilities) for (proportions of) chargeable periods falling on or after 1 April 2015 (*section 76, Finance Act 2015*).

Under the Finance (No 2) Bill 2015, the rates are to be reduced as follows:

- 0.18% (short-term liabilities) and 0.09% (long-term equity and liabilities) from 1 January 2016.
- 0.17% (short-term liabilities) and 0.085% (long-term equity and liabilities) from 1 January 2017.
- 0.16% (short-term liabilities) and 0.08% (long-term equity and liabilities) from 1 January 2018.
- 0.15% (short-term liabilities) and 0.075% from (long-term equity and liabilities) 1 January 2019.
- 0.14% (short-term liabilities) and 0.07% (long-term equity and liabilities) from 1 January 2020.
- 0.10% (short-term liabilities) and 0.05% (long-term equity and liabilities) from 1 January 2021.

However, this will be (more than) offset by a new corporation tax surcharge (of 8%) for banks from 1 January 2016.

The levy is paid through the corporation tax quarterly instalment payments system and interest is chargeable on late payments. Groups are able to nominate a member to account for, and be primarily responsible for, the levy, although joint and several liability attaches to some other group members.

Provisions will apply to avoid double taxation where non-UK bank levies also apply, although details are not yet known in relation to territories other than France, Germany and The Netherlands.

The levy is not deductible for UK corporation tax purposes and anti-avoidance provisions may apply.

26. Are there any thresholds or exemptions?

If the amount of the chargeable equity and liabilities is no more than GB£20 billion, no levy is charged and no more steps are required.

Where the amount of chargeable equity and liabilities exceeds GB£20 million, it will be necessary to determine what percentage of the chargeable equity and liabilities are long-term equity and liabilities and what percentage are short-term liabilities. The amount on which the levy would otherwise be chargeable that falls within each category is reduced by that percentage of £20 billion. The result is that £20 billion of the chargeable equity and liabilities of the relevant group or relevant entity is exempt from the levy (*section 73 and Schedule 19, Paragraph 6 of the Finance Act 2011*).

The following are excluded from this calculation of the levy:

+ Tier one capital.
+ Certain "protected" deposits.
+ Financial Services Compensation Scheme (FSCS) liabilities.
+ Certain insurance liabilities.
+ Certain property-related revaluation reserves.
+ Deferred tax liabilities, current tax liabilities and liabilities in respect of the levy.
+ Retirement benefit liabilities.
+ Clients' money.
+ Liabilities backing currency notes.

- Sovereign repo and stock-lending liabilities.
- Certain liabilities representing cash collateral.

Liabilities may also be reduced for these purposes under specific netting rules and in relation to high quality liquid assets.

REFORM

27. Please summarise any proposals for reform that will impact on the taxation of finance transactions described above.

The annual levy banks pay on their balance sheets is to be reduced gradually, but an 8% surcharge on their profits will be introduced. On 8 July 2015 the Treasury said the bank levy would be cut from its current 0.21% to 0.1% in 2021, by which time it would apply to banks' UK balance sheets only. The new profit surcharge will start from 1 January 2016.

The annual investment allowance has changed four times since 2008 and is due to change again to GB£200,000 on 1 January 2016.

ONLINE RESOURCES

Practical Law Company

W uk.practicallaw.com

Description This website is maintained by Practical Law (Subscription only) providing the latest legal updates in your practice area.

Legislation.gov.uk

W www.legislation.gov.uk

Description This website is maintained by The National Archives on behalf of HM Government and publishes all UK legislation.

Taxation of Foreign domiciliaries

W www.foreigndomiciliaries.co.uk

Description This website provides comprehensive information about:

- Taxation of foreign domiciliaries
- Taxation of non-residents on UK income and assets
- Taxation of UK residents on foreign income and assets

Westlaw.co.uk

W www.westlaw.co.uk

Description This website is maintained by Thomson Reuters (Subscription only) providing the expert analysis with expert analysis and links to the key related content.

HM Revenue and Customs

W www.hmrc.gov.uk

Description This website contains manuals and guidance on the application of UK tax. The information is HMRC's views as to the interpretation and application of tax legislation and resources. HMRC's view of the law may not always be correct.

Gov.UK

W www.gov.uk

Description this is the website of the UK government. It provides information on government services.

Emma Chamberlain; Chris Whitehouse (Trust Taxation and Estate Planning 4th Edition) (published by Sweet & Maxwell).

Description: this book provides valuable guidance, and practical application on the taxation of trust.

Dicey Morris and Collins (on the Conflict of Laws, edited by Lord Collins of Mapesbury 15th Edition) (London: Sweet & Maxwell, 2012)

Summary of key succession regime provisions

Jurisdiction	Is there a forced heirship regime (or similar)?	Are there ways to avoid it?
UK	None	Not applicable.

Inheritance or gift tax

Jurisdiction	Is inheritance or gift tax paid on death?	How can liability for inheritance or gift tax be reduced?
UK	Yes. Relevant Property Trust. Qualifying IIP trust. Trust for bereaved minors:	• Using annual allowances. • Using gifts out of ordinary income. • Using a PET and then surviving seven years. • Using a bare trust. • Establishing a family limited liability partnership (LLP). • Ensuring that existing assets used in a trade or business qualifies for Business Property or Agricultural Property Relief. • Restructuring shareholding (income and capital shares). Income share

		cease to have value on death, therefore if held by senior shareholders on death the value of the shares are not taken into account having ceased on death.
		• Creating an immediate post-death interest trust.
		• Use of a pilot trust.
		• Making gifts that will not qualify as a disposal for IHT purposes e.g. Gift for the maintenance of family, or gift out of ordinary income.

Withholding tax requirement on interest on corporate debt, and the key exemptions

Jurisdiction	What is the withholding tax requirement on interest on corporate debt?	What are the key exemptions (ignoring double tax treaties)?	What is the rate?
UK (England and Wales)	UK tax must be withheld from payments of yearly interest with a UK source.	The key exemptions are as follows: • Quoted Eurobond exemption. • Recipient within charge to UK corporation tax on the interest. • Interest payable by a bank in the ordinary course of its business.	20%.

AUTHOR'S PROFILE

Dr Clifford J. Frank, LLM, PhD

Partner LEXeFISCAL LLP

T +44 (0)20 7887 1948

F + 44(0)20 7887 6001

E clifford@lexefiscal.com

W www.lexefiscal.com

Clifford is highly creative and full of get-up-and-go. After 38 years in the field, he still enjoys the daily challenges that Tax Attorneys face in today's evolving world of complex international business structure and personal wealth planning, he could not have chosen a more complex issue for his first book.

In 1990, together with a then-leading firm of solicitors in the UK, he successfully represented Saudi Arabian Airlines in a complex tax compliance issue. His firm was the first firm outside of HMRC appointed to operate an ad-hoc tax collection scheme. In HMRC v M (1994), Clifford represented M in a cross-border tax investigation that crossed several borders including Switzerland, resulting in M's tax liability being reduced from £2.6m to £74,000.

In 2005, he completed his Masters in International Tax and in 2008 a Higher Diploma in International

Arbitration from London University. Clifford joined LEXeFISCAL, Legal and Tax Advisors in 2010 and became a partner in 2012. In 2015 he was awarded a doctorate from Barclay School of Law,

Some of the recent transactions

- *Acting for seller in share sale, involved de-grouping issues and properties held outside the UK transferred to the UK: GB£6.1 million.*
- *Reorganisation of international group for royalty planning: GB£26 million.*
- *National Crime Agency investigation: GB£1.3 million.*
- *Acting for creditors group in GLA, action against an insolvent group: GB£6.4 million.*
- *Inheritance tax planning/cross-border Cyprus, Jersey and UK.*
- *Representing clients in HMRC fraud investigation, involving non-resident companies.*
- *Incorporating property investment partnership resulting in SDLT savings of GB£560,000.*
- *EIS application for business operating in central Africa, in bio-fuel (renewable energy) to raise capital of GB£4 million.*
- *Restructuring real estate portfolio MKV £64m resulting in tax savings of £1.1m and IHT savings of £4m.*
- *Consulting major Italian Merchant bank on establishing UK interim holding company.*
- *Restructuring GB£1 million of foreign loans bringing the same onshore, with a 10% tax charge.*

Qualifications. LLM (tax), 2005; HDipICArb 2008, London University; Certified Mediator, Regent University, London; Cavalla International University (Barclay School of Law) Minnesota (USA)-2015: Degree of Doctor of Juridical Science (International Financial

Law) and Degree of Doctor of Philosophy in Law (Honoris Causa) PhD, 2015

LLB (Part complete)

Awards

2015 Leading Adviser - Acquisition International

2016 Contributor - Practical Law

Areas of practice. International and domestic taxation; trust; corporate law; arbitration and mediation.

Publications
- *3 Ways to Settle Your Tax: Staying in Switzerland and Preserving Your Anonymity.*
- *REIT' s creating value & liquidity from a property portfolio tax efficiently.*
- *Why me? A tax investigation, publication September 2016.*

CONTRIBUTORS' PROFILE

ANGELO CHIRULLI, ACA (UK & ITALY), CIPD

Professional qualifications. CTA partly qualified (2015); CIPD (2015); ACA (Italy/UK); Certified Payroll and Employment Law Consultant (Italy) (2001).

Non-professional qualifications. Masters in Business Administration (Italy) (2003); Masters Degree in Economics (2002).

Printed in May 2016

© 2016 LEXeFISCAL LLP.

www.ingramcontent.com/pod-product-compliance
Lightning Source LLC
Chambersburg PA
CBHW070329190526
45169CB00005B/1816